PICTURE LIBRARY

UNDERSEA MACHINES

PICTURE LIBRARY
UNDERSEA MACHINES

R. J. Stephen

Franklin Watts

London   New York   Sydney   Toronto

© 1986 Franklin Watts Ltd

First published in Great Britain
   1986 by
Frankin Watts Ltd
12a Golden Square
London W1R 4BA

First published in the USA by
Franklin Watts Inc
387 Park Avenue South
New York
N.Y. 10016

First published in Australia by
Franklin Watts
14 Mars Road
Lane Cove
2066 NSW

UK ISBN: 0 86313 419 X
US ISBN: 0-531-10187-8
Library of Congress Catalog Card
Number 85-52093

Printed in Italy
by Tipolitografia G. Canale & C. S.p.A. - Turin

Designed by
Barrett & Willard

Photographs by
N. S. Barrett Collection
British Telecom
BUE Services
Conoco
Scicon
Shell Photographic Service
US Navy
Woods Hole Oceanographic Institution
ZEFA/Photri

Illustration by
Rhoda & Robert Burns
Stuart Willard

Technical Consultant
Mike Borrow

Series Editor
N. S. Barrett

Contents

Introduction

Special machines are needed for working deep under water. The pressure of the water on humans and machines gets greater the farther down you go. It is also dark and very cold.

There are several kinds of machines, or submersibles, used for underwater work. Some have a crew, but most are unmanned.

△ A manned submersible ready to be launched from its "mother" ship. It has lights, cameras and scientific instruments for underwater research. It also has a "transfer skirt," at the bottom. This may be used for rescue work – to pick up crew members of a submarine, for example.

Undersea machines have many purposes. Scientific machines are used for exploring the seabed and carrying out experiments. Unmanned, or robot, submersibles check cables and pipelines. Submersibles have also been built for rescue work.

△ Manned and un-manned submersibles together on the seabed. The top one (RCV) is a remotely controlled vehicle used for observation. It has a TV camera operated from the surface. The PC1805 has a crew of two and is used to support divers from oil rigs.

A manned submersible

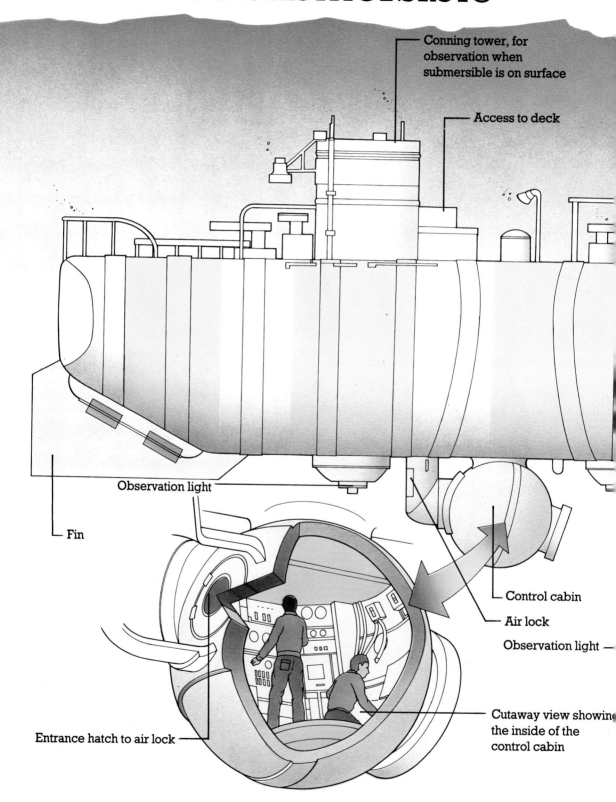

Conning tower, for observation when submersible is on surface

Access to deck

Observation light

Fin

Control cabin

Air lock

Observation light —

Entrance hatch to air lock

Cutaway view showing the inside of the control cabin

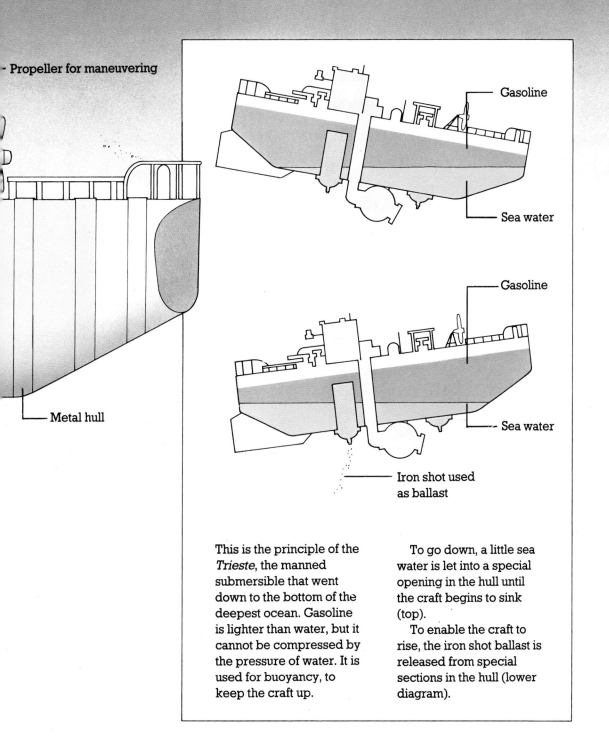

Propeller for maneuvering

Metal hull

Gasoline

Sea water

Gasoline

Sea water

Iron shot used
as ballast

This is the principle of the *Trieste*, the manned submersible that went down to the bottom of the deepest ocean. Gasoline is lighter than water, but it cannot be compressed by the pressure of water. It is used for buoyancy, to keep the craft up.

To go down, a little sea water is let into a special opening in the hull until the craft begins to sink (top).

To enable the craft to rise, the iron shot ballast is released from special sections in the hull (lower diagram).

Deep-sea diving

The biggest problem encountered in deep-sea diving is the pressure of the water. To work at depths greater than about 100 ft (30 m), divers have to breathe a special gas mixture of oxygen and helium. With this, they can go down as far as 1,500 ft (450 m) below the surface.

In atmospheric diving suits, divers can work at depths of 2,000 ft (600 m). To go down any farther, special machines are needed.

▽ Having changed into their clothes, divers relax in a decompression chamber while their bodies adjust to the lower pressure (left). After working for long periods at great depths, divers have to spend up to eight days in a decompression chamber.

This special diving suit, called "Jim," keeps the diver at normal air pressure (below). As a result, decompression is not needed.

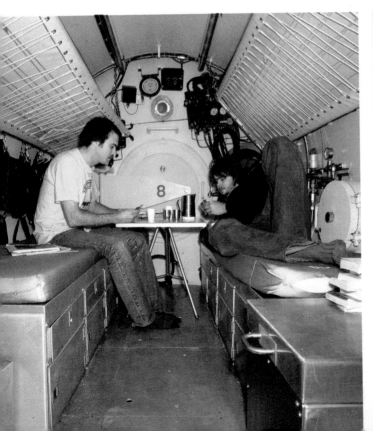

It is dangerous for a diver to rise too fast, before the body can adjust to the change in pressure. The air in the blood expands and forms bubbles. This causes decompression sickness, or the "bends."

To avoid getting the bends, divers make scheduled stops on their way back to the surface. For lengthy stops, this may be done in a special decompression chamber.

△ Divers relax in an underwater laboratory called a habitat. Several of these were built to study the effects of living underwater for long periods, perhaps a few months. The air pressure inside habitats is kept equal to that of the surrounding water. So the divers, or aquanauts, can stay outside the habitat for as long as their air tanks last.

Manned submersibles

Most manned submersibles have a crew of two or three. They are usually launched from a "mother" ship. They carry a mass of scientific equipment both inside and out.

Many submersibles have a "diver lockout chamber." This is separate from the rest of the submersible. When the diver opens the hatch to the sea, water cannot get into the main compartment.

△ Inside a submersible. The hatch separates the pilot compartment, which stays at normal air pressure, from the diver lockout chamber, at the front of the picture. When a diver goes out, the lockout chamber is pumped up with air to a high pressure. This prevents sea water coming in.

▷ A diver emerging from the lockout chamber.

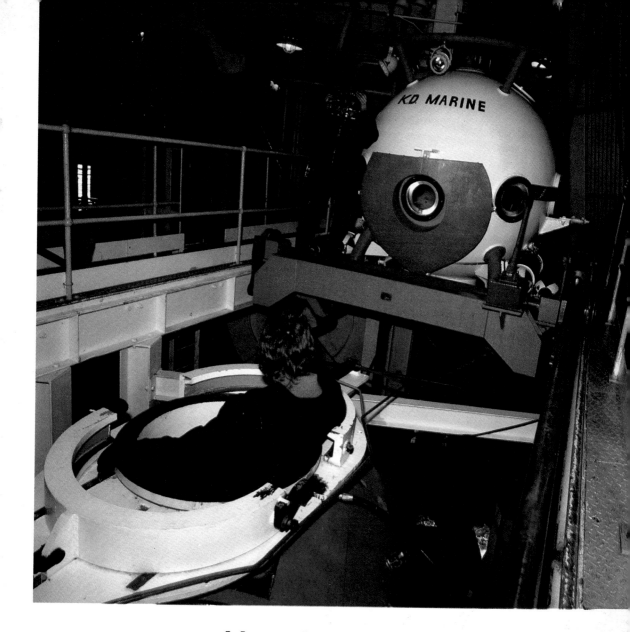

△ A diving chamber, or diving bell, being prepared for a deep dive off an oil platform.

◁ A manned submersible being launched. It has a special device for laying telephone cable under the seabed.

Manned submersibles are used chiefly for underwater engineering work. Lockout divers carry out repair and maintenance work on oil rigs, pipelines and cables.

Other uses of manned craft include scientific research.

△ A manned submersible about to dive.

◁ A special lifeboat being lowered into the sea from the side of an oil production platform. It contains a decompression chamber for use if the platform itself has to be evacuated in an emergency.

Unmanned submersibles

Most routine underwater work can now be done automatically by unmanned submersibles. These remotely operated vehicles (ROV) are used for inspection, maintenance and straightforward repair work.

Unmanned submersibles are also used for scientific and technical research. They study the oceans and sea life, and survey the seabed.

▽ The RCV (Remote Camera Video) is a small remotely operated vehicle. It may be operated from a surface vessel or from an oil platform. It is used for visual inspection and diver support, enabling surface control to keep a watchful eye on operations.

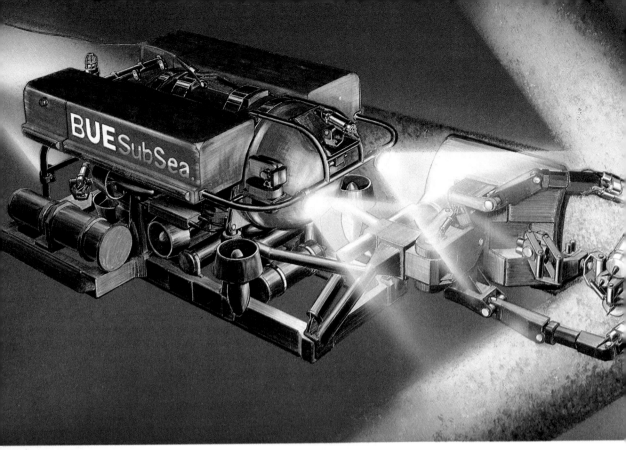

△ A remotely
controlled machine
inspects joints in an
underwater structure.
These "robots" produce
color video pictures and
take measurements
with their sensors. Some
of these machines can
be used to carry out
simple repairs and
maintenance tasks with
manipulator arms.

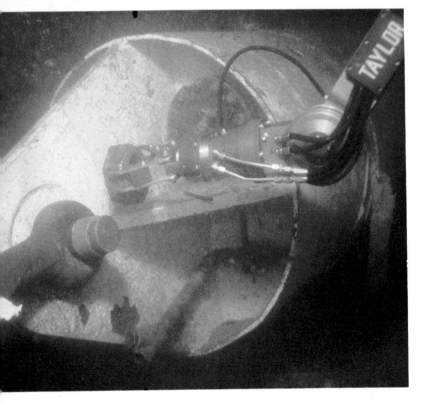

◁ A manipulator arm
unscrewing a $5\frac{1}{2}$ in
(14 cm) nut from an
underwater pipeline.

△ Consub 2 being
lowered into the sea
from its mother vessel.
This is an unmanned
submersible used for
pipeline inspection.

▷ A photograph
received from a
pipeline inspection
vehicle. Apart from the
plant life and debris on
the ocean floor, it shows
clearly the damage to
the concrete coating of
the pipe.

Offshore oil operations make great use of unmanned submersibles. Drilling rigs, production platforms and pipelines all need regular inspection and maintenance. More and more of the routine diving work has now been taken over by remotely controlled machines.

△ The Seadog submersible has crawler tracks for moving along the sea-bed. It is used for burying, inspecting and repairing underwater cable at depths down to 1,000 ft (300 m). It is linked by a line to a cable ship, from which it is controlled.

▷ A remote maintenance vehicle (RMV) specially designed for use with a particular oil installation, the underwater manifold center (UMC), shown below. The RMV travels along a track inside the UMC and is controlled from a surface vessel.

▽ The UMC being held by a tug before being submerged. It is used to collect and pass on oil to the chief production platform.

Underwater rescue

Submersibles are used for search and rescue work under the sea. There are robot search vehicles and manned rescue submersibles. Some are launched from surface vessels. One type of rescue submersible is carried on a submarine, which takes it under the water.

▽ The manned submersible LR5 on contract to the British Navy for rescue work. Personnel from military submarines in distress may be transferred to the LR5 from the escape tower by way of a transfer skirt.

△ The DSRV, or Deep Submergence Rescue Vehicle, is used by the US Navy for rescue work. The picture shows a DSRV attached to a submarine, which carries it down to the submarine in distress.

◁ An underwater view of a DSRV. It can rescue 24 men at a time, and go down to a depth of over 3,500 ft (1,000 m).

Finding the *Titanic*

The *Titanic,* the greatest ocean liner of its day, sank in 1912, when it hit an iceberg. Ever since then, people have dreamed of salvaging the famous ship.

This dream came nearer to reality in 1985, when a joint US – French mission found it. An unmanned submersible was sent down, about 13,000 ft (4,000 m) to the bottom of the ocean. It took pictures of the well-preserved wreck.

▽ An artist's impression of the sinking of the *Titanic,* on its very first voyage. More than 1,500 of the 2,200 passengers and crew were lost. The liner went down in the Atlantic Ocean, about 500 miles (800 km) south of Newfoundland, Canada, on a voyage between England and the United States.

▷ The *Alvin*, a manned submersible scheduled to explore the *Titanic* wreck.

▽ Anchor chains and other features on the *Titanic*'s deck can be seen in this ghostly picture, one of many taken by a robot craft when the wreck was first discovered.

Future robots

Scientists are continually improving robot submersibles. Computers and mechanical "hands" are replacing people for nearly all undersea work. What used to be science fiction is rapidly becoming fact.

One of the most advanced ideas is a submersible called SPUR. This stands for Scicon Patrolling Undersea Robot. Scicon is the group of scientists and technicians who designed the submersible.

△ A model of SPUR, which is about 33 ft (10 m) long and 6 ft (1.8 m) wide and high. It will be able to navigate by itself, avoid collisions, and select and attack targets.

SPUR is an "intelligent" robot designed for naval operations around the beginning of the next century. It will have both defensive and attacking roles and will also be used for peaceful purposes.

A squadron of SPURs could guard against underwater attack. They could also fire torpedoes and other weapons. SPURs could relieve ships and submarines of some of their most dangerous and costly tasks.

▽ An underwater view of SPUR. It looks simple, but contains detecting, steering and communications equipment, cameras, weapons and a very powerful computer. Its high-speed engine gives it a cruising speed of 12 knots (13.8 miles) and an attack speed of 50 knots (60 miles). It has legs for standing on the seabed.

The story of undersea machines

Diving for treasures

People have dived for treasures under the sea for thousands of years. The first divers had no breathing apparatus to help them. They dove for shells, sponges or pearls.

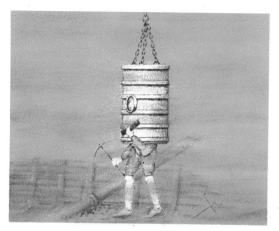

△ Lorena's diving bell of the early 1500s.

The first diving bells

The first devices that allowed divers to breathe underwater were diving bells. Real bells made of metal were used. Later they were made of wood, kept down with lead weights. The bell shape is open to the water at the bottom, but the greater air pressure inside keeps the water out. Air from the surface may be supplied from a hose. The first reliable record of a practical diving bell was published in 1531, although diving bells are known

to have been used for hundreds of years before that. This bell was made by an Italian called Lorena.

One of the most successful of the early diving bells was built by the astronomer Edmund Halley, who gave his name to the famous comet. It was made of wood, lined with lead. Divers could work outside for brief periods.

△ Halley's diving bell of 1690. Divers breathed air through a tube. Fresh air was sent down in barrels.

Deep-sea research

For deep-sea diving, strong machines are needed to withstand the great pressures. The first apparatus used to explore the ocean depths was the bathysphere, in 1930. It was a heavy steel ball, lowered from a ship by cables. It contained oxygen tanks, and was big enough for one scientist, sealed inside. He could communicate with the surface by telephone. Larger bathyspheres were built, but their big disadvantage was that they could not move about.

An improvement on the bathysphere was the bathyscaphe, first tested in 1948. This could be maneuvered up and down by the occupants.

The first manned submersibles were built in the 1960s. These can travel freely under water and do not need to be linked to their support ship.

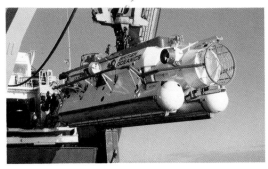

△ The LR3, a commercial manned submersible, being launched by its support ship. It is made of glass reinforced plastic, and can carry a crew of four.

△ The *Alvin*, built in 1964, was the first manned deep-ocean submersible.

Commercial craft

Submersibles have been greatly improved in the 1970s and 1980s, and most are now used for commercial work.

The latest manned submersibles are made of glass reinforced plastic. They have ample space for a crew of three or four plus a great deal of equipment and instruments. Divers can leave the craft to work outside.

Most commercial jobs, however, are now done by unmanned submersibles, operated by remote control.

△ Most undersea work is now done by remotely controlled machines.

Facts and records

△ The record-breaking *Trieste*.

Going down

Two Americans, the naturalist William Beebe and the engineer Otis Barton, built the first bathysphere. It was a steel ball nearly 13 ft (4 m) in diameter, without any joints. The steel was $1\frac{1}{2}$ in (38 mm) thick.

In 1934, they went down to a record depth of 3,031 ft (924 m) in a bathysphere.

Deeper and deeper

The first bathyscaphe was designed by a Swiss professor, the balloonist Auguste Piccard, in the late 1940s. He then built a more successful one in Italy, called the *Trieste*. It was bought by the US Navy for research, and equipped with a new deep diving sphere. In 1960, Piccard's son Jacques and Lieutenant Donald Walsh of the US Navy descended to the deepest part of the ocean floor, known as the Challenger Deep. This is in the Pacific Ocean, and is about 36,000 ft (10,900 m) down.

Glossary

Aquanaut
Name sometimes given to a person who works under water.

Atmospheric diving suit
A special diving suit in which the pressure is kept at that of the air at sea level. No decompression is needed when the diver returns to the surface from a dive.

Bathyscaphe
An underwater craft used to explore the ocean depths. Bathyscaphes could be moved up and down by their occupants, but had very little other maneuverability.

Bathysphere
A heavy steel ball lowered from a ship so that scientists inside could study ocean life and make scientific observations.

Bends
Sickness caused by a rapid change of pressure in the lungs due to coming up too fast from a dive.

Decompression chamber
A sealed room or compartment where divers gradually adapt their bodies to normal pressure again.

Diver lockout chamber
Compartment in a submersible from which a diver can leave.

Diving bell
A submersible from which divers work.

Habitat
An underwater laboratory designed to study the effects of living in deep water for long periods.

Manipulator arm
A mechanical arm. On manned submersibles, it is operated from the inside; on unmanned submersibles, by remote control.

ROV
Remotely operated vehicle.

Submersible
Most underwater machines might be called submersibles, but the word usually refers to one that can travel freely without being linked to a support ship.

Transfer skirt
A mating device on a submersible, used for transferring people or equipment to or from another submerged vehicle.

Index

32